CHAMPIONSHIP
NHRA
DRAG RACING

Winston Drag Racing

...NSHIP DRAG RACING...

...g Racing

PONTIAC

AUSTRALIA

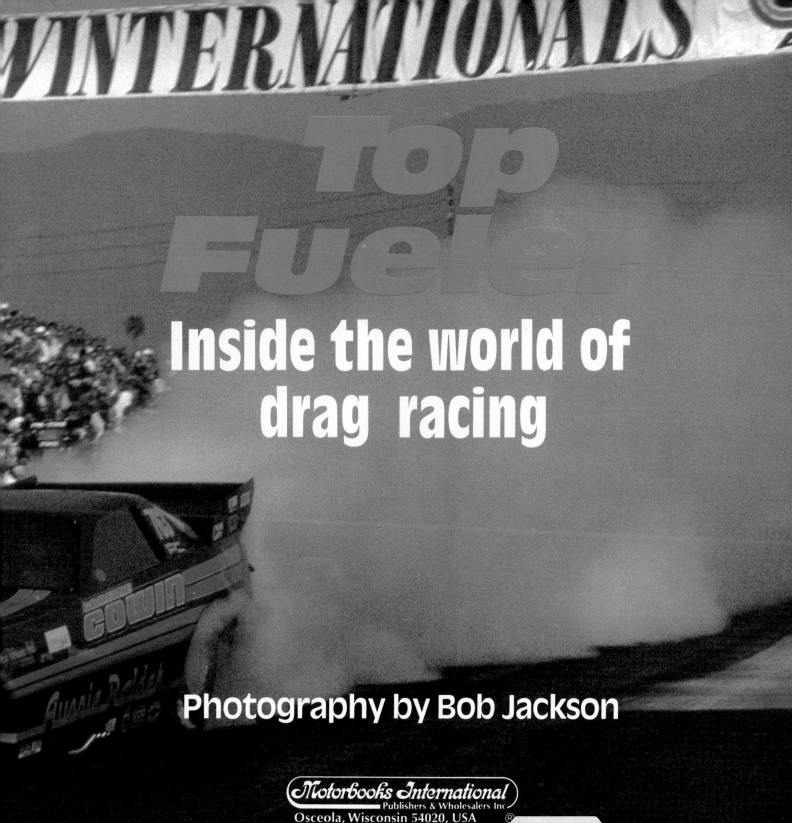

Top Fueler

Inside the world of drag racing

Photography by Bob Jackson

Motorbooks International
Publishers & Wholesalers Inc
Osceola, Wisconsin 54020, USA

First published in 1987 by Motorbooks
International Publishers & Wholesalers
Inc, PO Box 2, 729 Prospect Avenue,
Osceola, WI 54020 USA

Printed and bound in Hong Kong

The information in this book is true and
complete to the best of our knowledge.
All recommendations are made without any guarantee on the part of the
author or publisher, who also disclaim
any liability incurred in connection with
the use of this data or specific details

**Library of Congress
Cataloging-in-Publication Data**
Jackson, Bob
  Top fueler.

  1. Automobiles, Racing.   I. Title.
TL236.J24 1987 629.2'28 87-12266
ISBN 0-87938-250-3

Motorbooks International books are
also available at discounts in bulk
quantity for industrial or sales-promo-
tional use. For details write to Special
Sales Manager at the Publisher's
address

Acknowledgments

Shooting the pictures for a book like this would be impossible without access to areas where the action is taking place. I'd like to thank Tammy Ferrell, media relations manager for NHRA, for allowing me that access, and for providing me with materials that helped fill the technical gaps.

I'd also like to thank Sam Cho, whose magic potions in the photo lab produced the colors that helped bring these monsters to life.

Contents

Introduction

There's no other sound like it in motor sports.
There may be no other sound like it in the world!
We're talking about the supercharged, 3,000 hp, nitromethane-burning Top Fuel drag racing engine.

So distinctive is its sound, that from a half mile away—at a drag strip already ripe with the sound of dozens of engines—the freshly fired Top Fueler announces its presence with a resonance that pierces the air and grabs the attention in much the same manner other Kings of the Jungle must!

It's difficult to describe the sound of the Top Fueler to one who's never heard it. Part scream, part roar; it is all awesome power!

And while the Top Fueler's sound may be tough to verbally picture, its sensation is brutally simple: It does not surround you; it goes right through you!

As the Top Fueler goes past, propelling car and driver over one-quarter mile in less than 5.5 seconds—at speeds of more than 270 mph—your face shimmers, your eardrums reverberate to the point of pain and your insides rumble!

And it's beautiful! You can't wait for the next car to come past!

The major sanctioning body for automobile drag racing in the United States is the National Hot Rod Association (NHRA).

Founded by Wally Parks, in 1951, the NHRA conducts a series of National and Regional events across the United States, from January through October each year. National events include the Winternationals, in Pomona, California; Gatornationals; Southern Nationals; Cajun Nationals; Springnationals; Grand

National Molson, in Canada; Summernationals; Mile-High Nationals; Northstar Nationals; U.S. Nationals in Indianapolis, Indiana, on Labor Day weekend; Keystone Nationals; Chief Auto Parts Nationals; Fallnationals; and, finally, the Winston World Finals back in Pomona, where the championship trail started.

Points gathered at these official NHRA races lead to the coronation of World Champions in nine classes.

Six of those classes are considered "Sportsman." Only three classes are considered "Professional." And while Pro Stock cars continue to improve in terms of sophistication, speed and fan interest, the Top Fuel funny cars and Top Fuel dragsters are the unchallenged super stars of the sport.

A typical National event includes three days of qualification runs. Cars are timed, from a standing start, for the quarter mile; clocking an elapsed time (ET). A speed trap at the end of the quarter mile also catches the speed they're going at that point, and assigns them a top speed.

The sixteen fastest cars—by elapsed time, not top speed—qualifying for Sunday's program of head-to-head, single-elimination match races. Three rounds of racing produce two drivers who'll battle for the championship of the meet.

So, if you have your ear plugs in place, come along as we tour drag strips all across the country: tracking the automobile world's King of the Beasts, the Top Fueler!

To the drags

Next page

The Top Fuel dragster is called The King of the Sport. They've also been called "slingshots," and "rails." NHRA rules call for a minimum wheelbase of 180 inches; and a minimum weight, with driver, of 1,800 pounds. As this is written, the world standing-start quarter-mile record ET for Top Fuel dragster is 5.22 seconds. The top speed record is 278.55 mph.

The first order of business is to bring the race car out of its transporter. It must be done carefully; there's a big investment here. This car costs somewhere in the neighborhood of $75,000; and it would be tough to lose it while on the trailer. Most of the major teams use eighteen-wheelers for transporters. The purchase price and cost of equipping these beauties can run to as much as $200,000! But the touring drag racer may not see home for months; so, this is his home. The totally self-contained trailer may carry a couple of spare engines; possibly, a spare car; and enough machinery to do any repair imaginable.

9

Two parachutes are mandatory on Top Fuel cars. They're packed in the silver bags between the wheels. The rear tires may be no wider than seventeen inches, with a maximum circumference of 114 inches. A typical Goodyear rear tire might be 36x17.

The supercharged Top Fuel engine is limited to 500 cubic inches. A quick scan of entries in an NHRA National reveals the most popular engines are Dodge hemis, or their variations, constructed by famous drag race engine builder Keith Black. Depending on the team's budget, it may start the year with three complete engines, at approximately $35,000 apiece. Provided the team doesn't put something through their sides (like a stray rod, or something), with replacement components, the blocks will last the season. There's a lot of aluminum in the engine block and its component parts.

Funny car

The Top Fuel funny car shares equal—or, perhaps, better-than-equal—billing with the dragster. Funny cars have a couple of aliases, too. They're called "floppers," referring to the body's action in allowing driver access. And they've been called "The Plastic Fantastics," alluding to their fiberglass body construction. The funny car must weigh at least 2,050 pounds, with driver; and it's allowed a wheelbase from 100 inches to 125 inches. As this is written, the world standing-start quarter-mile record ET for Top Fuel funny car is 5.48 seconds. The top speed record is 268.09 mph.

The funny car's fuel tank carries approximately eighteen gallons; and, while not required, fuel cells (rubberized bags inside the aluminum tank to help inhibit fire) are recommended by the NHRA. The red bottles on either side of the fuel tank are fire extinguishers. These are very important to the funny car driver, since he's sitting behind the engine, surrounded by a body made of very flammable fiberglass.

The funny car engine is almost identical to that used in the dragster; it, too, is limited to 500 cubic inches. This engine is equipped with a brand-new, mandatory safety device: the "blower bag." Some of the greatest potential for damage and injury—to both driver and race fan—came from blower explosions and "shrapnel," when the supercharger was torn from the engine at great speed. Constructed of the same material as used in flak jackets, the bag consists of the black shroud on top, and the silver straps which hold the engine components in one "package," just in case.

Chute and wing

Parachutes, besides being mandatory, are necessary to help stop the Top Fueler. Most drag strips allow less than one-half mile past the finish line in which to brake a car that may have reached speeds of more than 270 mph! The ever-safety-conscious NHRA, where possible, has added some refinements to this "run-out" area, in the event parachutes malfunction or are burned off in an engine fire. There may be a strip-wide sand pit, allowing much of the speed to be scrubbed off and, finally, a net similar to those used to catch run-away jets on aircraft carriers.

The crew attaches the airfoil, or wing, to the car. Drag racing is just like any other form of motor sport: The challenge is transferring the tremendous power generated by the engine to the ground. The airfoil helps create the down-draft needed to help the car "stick" to the drag strip.

Sponsor

Sponsorship is a major part of the game of drag racing, and not just for the drivers, either. The R. J. Reynolds Tobacco Company, with its Winston cigarettes, is a major underwriter, along with the NHRA, of drag racing's prize purses. Castrol, Chief Auto Parts, Motorcraft, Budweiser and Quaker State are also taking on National-event co-sponsorships. Besides support from sponsors, drivers earn "contingency" money from those companies whose decals they carry on the car: provided they win! Sponsors are the backbone of drag racing.

Fuel

Since it's impossible to take warm-up laps in a Top Fueler, most cars are briefly fired up in the pits. Here, drag racing legend Don "The Snake" Prudhomme directs his crew to go easy on an adjustment during his "run" in the pits.

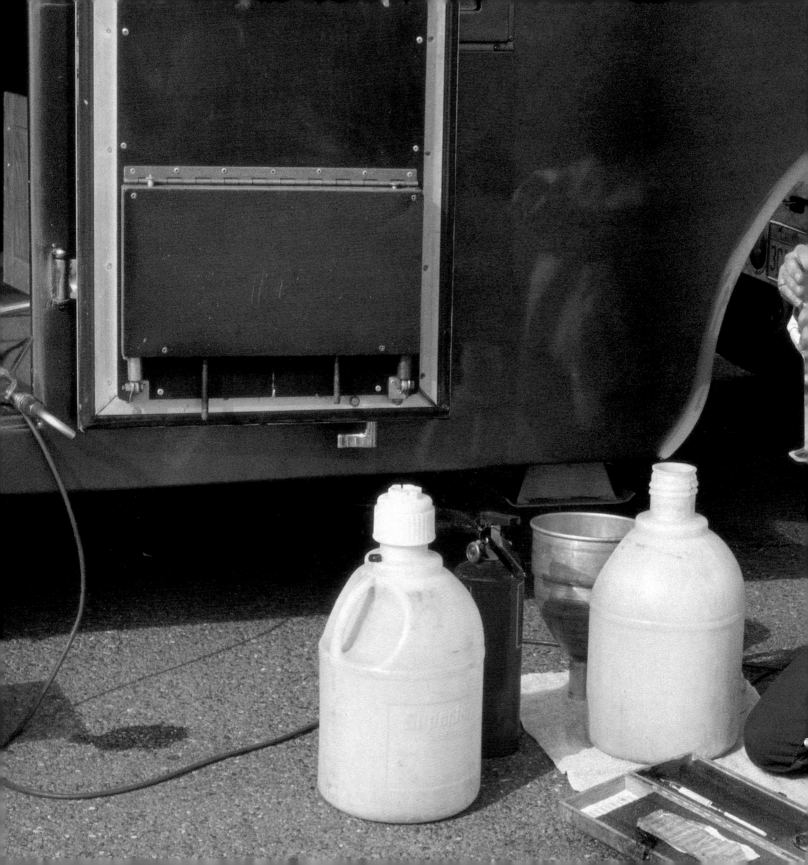

This dragster driver carefully checks the ratio of nitromethane to methanol, the components making up the Top Fueler's fuel. Most drivers use 90-95 percent "nitro" to 5-10 percent methanol, an alcohol. Nitromethane is called "liquid gold" for a very good reason: It costs approximately $1,600 for one fify-five-gallon drum!

Tires

Tire pressure is checked on a funny car. The Top Fuelers' tires are actually "a tire in a tire." This is what accounts for the crinkling of the sidewall you may notice when the car is rolling at slow speeds. Each set of rear tires costs approximately $250. If lucky, the crew may get seven "runs" (burnouts, plus quarter-mile passes) per set.

This is the traditional dragster front-end. These used to be called "bicycle" tires, because of their skinny, spoked configuration. But NHRA has outlawed spoked wheels. Now, they're made of cast-aluminum. Again, the airfoil between the wheels helps "glue" the car to the drag strip.

Next page
The Great Innovator, Don "Big Daddy" Garlits, began running this front-end during the 1986 season. It consists of a solid "pod," and employs tiny jet fighter airplane wheels. Garlits' theory is "go as low as possible." This configuration makes his dragster look very much like an arrow. To his competitors, it also appears to travel very much at an arrow's speed!

Cage and airflow

Another of the NHRA safety features is the padded roll cage protecting the driver's head. Roll cages are often constructed of 4130 chromemoly, with an outside diameter of 1⅝ inches and a wall thickness of 0.083 inch.

Another of Big Daddy's streamlining ideas is being picked up by some of the other drivers: the enclosed cockpit. This is the version being employed by Shirley Muldowney, another of drag racing's legends. Note the tastefully appointed rearview mirror, in matching "hot pink." The mirror's basic function is to help her find her way back from burnouts, but it could also be used to keep track of her trailing competitors.

Next page
Yet another streamlining idea is this enclosed cockpit pod, employed by Gary Ormsbey's Castrol-sponsored dragster.

High tech

This is a close-up look at the blower bag. As mentioned earlier, the straps keep everything together, kind of like a rolling trash compactor. To this point, the blower bag appears to be working, as designed—there has been an absence of dangerous "shrapnel" coming from blown engines.

What can you say about the cleanliness and efficiency of the driver's compartment in Gary Ormsbey's dragster? Drag racers combine elegance with efficiency about as well as can be done, don't they?

This is a funny car, sans "car." Rules say the
funny car body must resemble "A 1982 or
later model-year coupe, sedan or station
wagon body of a type originally mass-
produced by an automobile manufacturer."
One of the funny car's appeals is the
beautiful color schemes employed. Grilles,
headlights and taillights are painstakingly
painted on. Despite the intricate detail, and
substantial look, the funny car body may
weigh as little as 100 pounds!

Staging lane

It's time to get to the staging lanes, the area where competitors line up prior to entering the drag strip. Last-minute adjustments and consultations take place while the cars are waiting to be called. Late on the final day of qualifying, or on the final Sunday of the meet, these adjustments may take on a frantic air.

Don Garlits eases himself into the confines of his cockpit. You can see the plastic canopy that encloses him tilted forward to give him access to the driver's compartment. The dragster drivers' suits are usually less bulky than those of the funny car pilots; more like the Indy or stock car driver would wear.

This funny car competitor fastens the chin strap on his helmet. With the engine practically in his face, the funny car driver used to wear a helmet device that looked much like a gas mask. But helmet technology has advanced to where the stock safety helmet is sufficient. Top Fuel drivers wear some type of fire suit, usually made of Nomex, or a similar material.

Joe Amato, one of the current super stars of Top Fuel drag racing, has a chat with a crew member, and with his wife, while waiting in line. Joe's wife performs an indispensable job when she realigns his starting spot on the launch pad following a burnout.

Next page

Don "Big Daddy" Garlits, concentrates on the work ahead. Though Top Fuel drivers are "on" for just a few seconds, there's a lot to think about, and do. Wouldn't you like to have just a penny for each run Garlits has prepared for in his lifetime?

This dragster driver is strapped into his car. Cars with roll cages, which includes all Top Fuelers, must employ "quick-release" shoulder harnesses. There may be times when the driver has to vacate the premises in a hurry.

Start

Garlits' tow car pulls his car to the starting area. The tow cars are important. They head downtrack right after the car has made its pass, and are immediately available to the driver, along with the NHRA's Safety Safari, should he need help with anything.

The eyes tell the story, as this funny car driver awaits the starter's command to "fire 'em up!" If you're still trying to make the final sixteen, these can be anxious moments, indeed.

The blower's injectors are primed, the starter is put in place, and 3,000 horses leap to life with a sound like no other in auto racing. It's awesome, and then-some!

The driver rolls slowly through the water which has been poured on the pavement. This area used to be called a "bleach box," as bleach was used. Some crews still use a type of traction compound on each tire, just prior to the burnout, but most settle for the lubrication of plain ol' water. A couple of revolutions, and the racing slicks are completely wet, and ready to "fry."

The engine's revved, the clutch is popped, and the tires begin a spin that produces one of the great moments in auto sports, the burnout!

Next pages
While it is, indeed, a show—and Top Fuelers can be showmen—the purpose of the burnout is to heat the surface of the tires to the point of melting; thus, improving the traction of the tires on the pavement. Walk across the starting area in a loose-fitting shoe, following a burnout, and it's very likely you'll leave it on the pavement.

Combine the awesome shriek of the engine with the spectacle of rubber going up in smoke, and it's an experience that will "hook you" for a lot of years.

Next page

It's very important that the car return to the track it "laid" on the pavement; otherwise the burnout effort is wasted. The softened tires need the rubber cushion they produced for traction. Spotters, front and rear, help the driver align himself. The installation of reverse gear in Top Fuel cars, around 1980, has made these spotters' jobs a lot easier. They used to have to run down the track and push the cars back to the starting area!

There was a time when burnouts were "burnouts!" Crews were allowed to add flammable fluids to the bleach resulting in spectacular fire. The practice was allowed to continue, on some drag strips, into the early seventies, but "cooler heads" prevailed, and the potentially volatile burnout was outlawed.

The driver rolls slowly toward the "pre-staged" light, then to the "staged" light—the starting line—and awaits the green light. Meantime, the tensions and temperatures build!

Budweiser
Oldsmo
ston Drag Racing
Motorcraft
QUALITY PARTS
Bud

Launch

A perfect launch! There's not a trace of white tire smoke, the deadly sign that the car has lost traction. The car will go from zero to 60 in one-half second! It will go from zero to 100 in 1.1 seconds! From zero to 150 in 1.9 seconds! And from zero to 200 in three seconds! All this on its way to. . . .

Next page
A new world record for Top Fuel dragsters: 5.22 seconds in the quarter mile, at a top speed of 278 mph! This is awesome, defined! In order for a world record to be established, the driver must clock another time within one percent of his record-breaking time sometime during the event. The day after this run, Darrell Gwynn, in the Budweiser-sponsored car, clocked a run of 5.24 seconds; it was the back-up he needed!

Brake

The driver of this dragster feels the welcome pull of the parachute that will help brake him from the speed attained during the run.

Crew

Next page
The oil pan is swabbed with care. No one needs a stray piece of metal working its way into an area it wasn't designed for.

The driver's job is done. Now it's time for the crew members to go to work; and they'll have to hustle. This is Sunday, and there are only ninety minutes between rounds. That's right; ninety minutes in which to disassemble and reassemble a race car! It's not always necessary, but often, new pistons are needed. At about $60 a pop, with rings and rods, racing's an expensive business. If all goes well, meaning no blown engines, this crew may spend at least $10,000 during the event!

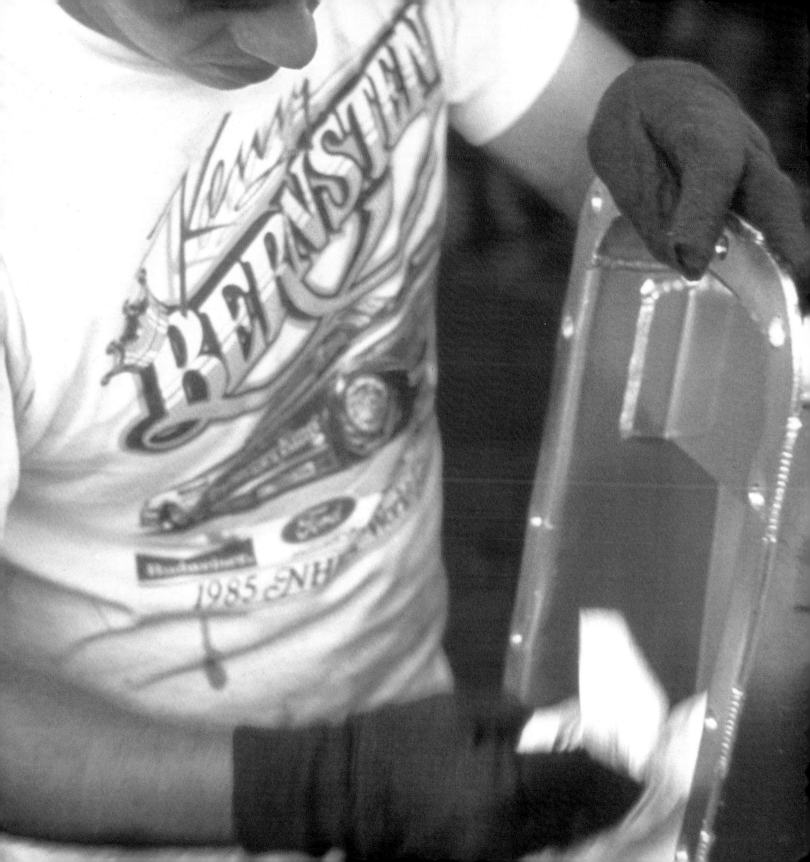

Next page
The crowd senses the excitement as the crew "thrashes" to get the car ready for the final round, and they press forward to share in the drama!

The Age of the Computer has reached Top Fuel drag racing. An on-board computer tracks such things as fuel flow, temperatures and shifting points—along with twenty-some other functions of the car—and the crew chief watches the readout to see what adjustments are needed! Sophistication? What makes you say that?

Next page
Incredible as it may seem, this car's cylinders are being rebored during this "intermission." If you took the family car in to have the work done these crews do in ninety minutes, the garage would have it for a minimum of two weeks!

The computer's indicated a jetting change. The mechanic needs to find one in a hurry!

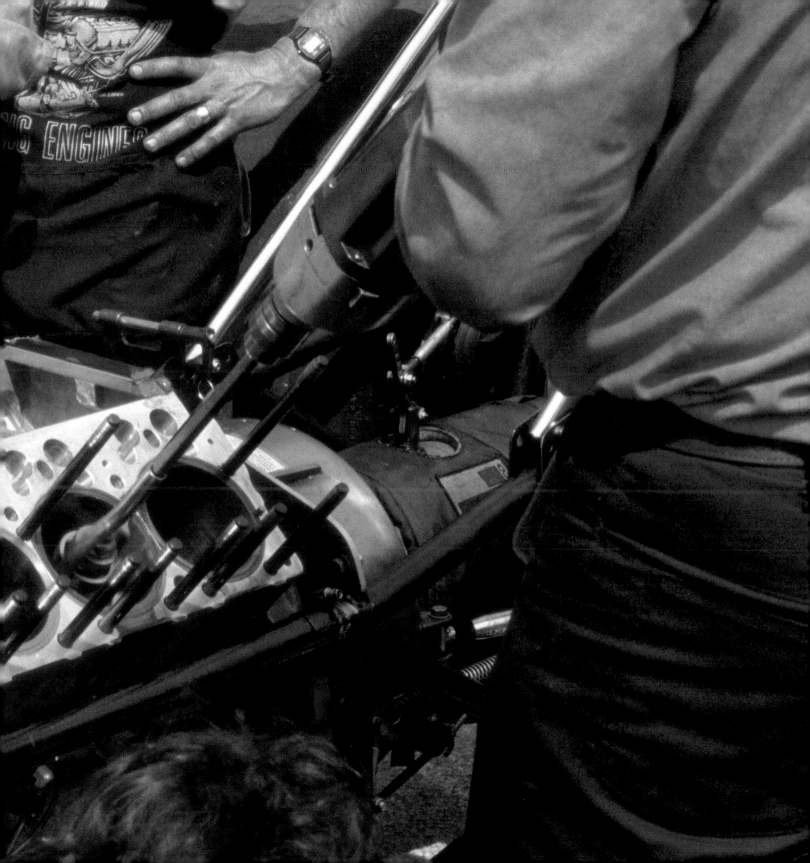

A head gasket is tapped in place, as "the beat goes on." Watching a top crew refurbish a Top Fueler is to see a kind of choreography. It's also what the medical school dean meant when he told his students that a critical artery needed to be sutured in two minutes for the patient to survive. "And you can do it, too, if you don't hurry," he told them. The bottom line to this entire exercise is that the driver trusts the job each of the crew members did enough to climb back in the car and go 270 mph again!

Kenny Bernstein, King of the current funny car crop, refills the tank with the liquid gold. Top Fuelers are not your basic high mpg automobiles; they gulp down an eighteen-gallon tankful with each run.

Close-up

Another run

The "old guard" visits with the new; Don Garlits, right, chats with Darrell Gwynn. Moments later, Gwynn covered the quarter-mile faster than anyone in drag racing history, a world record that Garlits has held at several points in his career.

Next page
It's back to the staging lanes, and this time the atmosphere is not as laid back as during qualifying rounds. The car needs help, and the crew isn't exactly sure where to look for it.

One last burnout. And the funny car driver hopes he's gotten a lane with "some good numbers" in it. If he hasn't, it's on to the next stop for yet another grab at the brass ring.

Next page
You can cut the tension with a knife, as the drivers ease into their pre-staged and staged positions, awaiting the "christmas tree's" countdown to green. Jam-packed stands along each side of the drag strip wait, too, as the drama builds!

While she's hardly in the twilight of her career, three-time World Champion Shirley Muldowney uses the sunset to complement the colors of her beautiful dragster.

Next page

Green light—it's a go! The combined noise of the two cars, side-by-side has nearby spectators cringing as the cars roar past. The drivers are undergoing g-forces that require them to complete the same FAA physical as jet pilots; they're under the same stress!

The Top Fuel funny car lopes, seemingly in discomfort, at the starting line. It was built to go fast, and is eager to get to work!

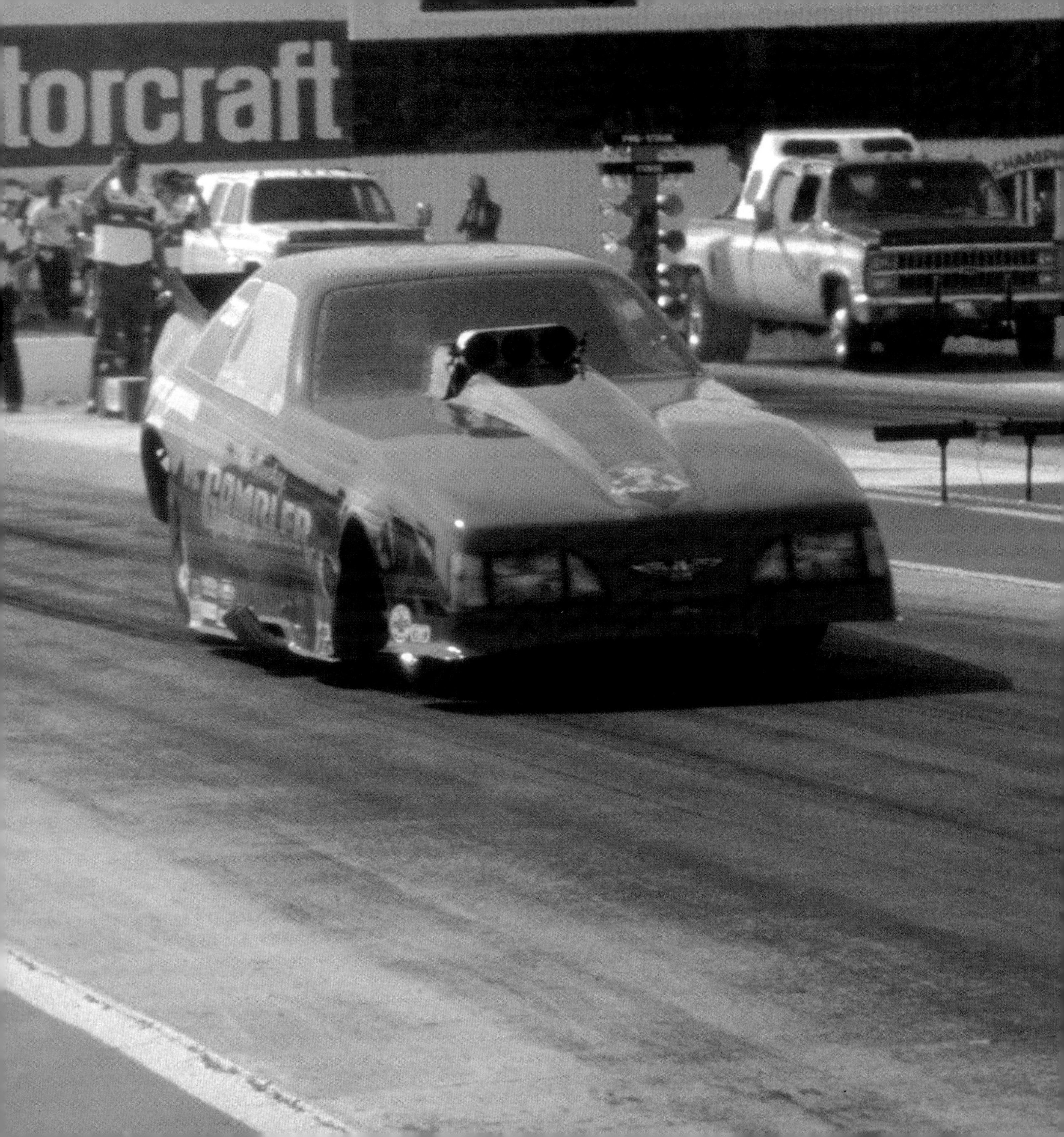
torcraft

Previous page

Another start. A classic "holeshot." The race doesn't always go to the "fast," sometimes it goes to the "quick." If it's to win this race, the blue car will have to "drive around" the red one, and this is not easily done! It's possible for a car with a faster ET, and top speed, to lose a side-by-side drag race. The first one down wins!

The starting line is not the only place on the drag strip the cars and drivers are under pressure. Look what speeds of 260-mph-plus do to fiberglass funny car body work. Talk about being puckered!

Next page
Occasionally, there's an engine fire at the "top end" of the track. Often, it's the result of oil leaking onto hot spots on the engine. With the engine being behind the dragster driver, chances of injury are lessened. But, occasionally, the fire burns the parachutes, making for an exciting ride through the "shut-off" area.

And the dragsters aren't at all immune to the resistance of the wind. Notice the seam that's developed in the side-panel of Shirley Muldowney's car, as the body is buffeted about. Imagine the shaking the driver's taking!

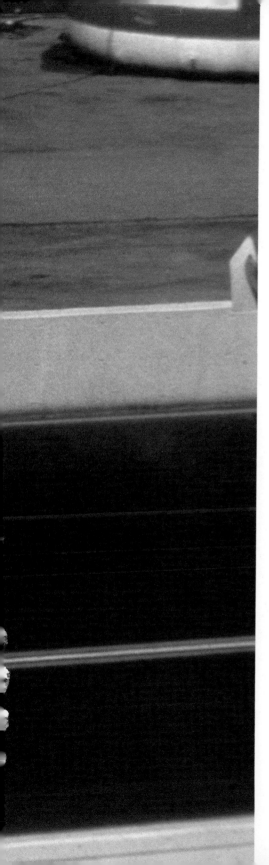

Next pages
It doesn't happen often, but sometimes a Top Fueler capsizes, as did Tim Morgan's car during the 1987 Winternationals, in Pomona, California. There was a happy ending, as Morgan's final roll left the car rightside up, and he walked away from it without a scratch!

Split second

And what happens most of all, is that the parachute pops out, braking another exhilarating, breath-taking, mind-blowing Top Fuel run, as on this neat, vintage front-engine dragster campaigned by Tony Nancy in the early seventies. As a certain beer commercial says, "It doesn't get any better." Does it?

Next pages
Far more often than not, between the drivers' skill and the NHRA's insistence on safe equipment, the finish line is the scene of some incredibly close racing. There's not much left to choose in either of these races, is there?